Sea Room

Other books
by Maria Flook

Reckless Wedding (poems)
Dancing with My Sister Jane (short stories)

Sea Room

Maria Flook

 Wesleyan University Press

Published by University Press of New England

Hanover and London

The University Press of New England

is a consortium of universities in New England dedicated to pub-
lishing scholarly and trade works by authors from member cam-
puses and elsewhere. The New England imprint signifies uniform
standards for publication excellence maintained without exception
by the consortium members. A joint imprint of University Press
of New England and a sponsoring member acknowledges the pub-
lishing mission of that university and its support for the dissemi-
nation of scholarship throughout the world. Cited by the Ameri-
can Council of Learned Societies as a model to be followed,
University Press of New England publishes books under its own
imprint and the imprints of Brandeis University, Brown Univer-
sity, Clark University, University of Connecticut, Dartmouth Col-
lege, University of New Hampshire, University of Rhode Island,
Tufts University, University of Vermont, and Wesleyan University

© 1990 by Maria Flook

Grateful acknowledgment is made to the editors of the following mag-
azines in which many of these poems first appeared: *The Agni Review*,
The Arts Journal, *Indiana Review*, *The Michigan Quarterly Review*, *The
Missouri Review*, *The New Criterion*, *Pacific Review*, and *Ploughshares*.
"1917" appeared originally as "The Orphan, 1917" in *The New Yorker*.
"The Improper Persons," "Affidavit," "Discreet," "The Sapling," "Against
Spring," and "Child Burial" appeared originally in *Poetry*.

"The Voice Lesson" is for Michael Burkard.

Printed in the United States of America

Library of Congress Cataloging-in-Publication Data
Flook, Maria.
Sea room / Maria Flook. — 1st ed.
    p.   cm. — (Wesleyan poetry)
    ISBN 0-8195-2183-3   ISBN 0-8195-1185-4 (pbk.)
    I. Title.   II. Series.
PS3556.L583S4   1990
811'.54 — dc20   89-14831
                                                      CIP

Wesleyan Poetry

54321

for John Skoyles

Contents

One

Affidavit

I was never touched by God,
not by the pastel leaflets
that fall from high windows.
I turned away from the voluptuous
entrance of a familiar building,
from the city, its numerical harbor
and sensual industries. Dreams
have cruel motives; sleep worries
both the decent and the wicked
who keep odd hours, so I walked out.
I hate to see myself in the darkened
glass of small bankruptcies,
and in the artificial snow
of empty shop fronts I just imagine
the lost inventories.
In factory sections, I walked too far
through informative mists and sulphurous
afterthought, whatever flashed
its impure memory upon the glazed air.
It is springtime, such untidy petals,
and the moon, soaked dark,
decays like a seed.
Let forlorn breezes examine my papers!
Let my naked sisters, my rooms, shiver.
And the bed, illegible mirror of my body,
have its sheet deepen over my stain.
I had inaccurate longings. I loved
only descriptions of love. Years,
in their casual way, began to pass.
Month after month rented my property.
Weeks arrived nervous
and left behind medicines.
A final, intimate day became hysterical
in my arms. Together we wept

the same twelve tears. After an hour
I folded those hands, I dragged the stone
of my childhood over so many names.

Household

There was a door floating on the water,
a white door with a glass knob.
All the envelopes swirled after
as if to find the proper letter slot.
It must be an admission of guilt
and the stiff responses following it.
There it goes, I said
to some fishermen's children
but they could not adjust their gaze.
They looked at the sea
as if it were a chore, a table
to be laid and cleared away.

At dark, I walked the frayed tideline,
a rope pulled taut
and then unraveling, one temperament
constantly dividing.
I saw the blurried harbor, and farther
the horizon, a plain immovable line.
Loose shingles of the stars
slapped down
but I saw no reflection
in the glassy surf, no light
from any windows on the shore.

The sea's worn roof slants
on and on, sometimes gabled
by a storm's harsh carpentry.
Even in a homeless calm
a whale beached here,
its baleen clattering
like window blinds askew
in the salty wind.
The hard past closed, nothing
remained but the anonymous life,
the forgiving krill.

Woodpecker

Shame doused him when he looked in
teased by my wallpaper, *Bird of Paradise*,
in a shade too rich. I was sewing
without needle or thread, a bit of vaudeville
I employed against the sweltering day
when nonsense overtakes strict privacy.
There, in the double glass of my vanity,
a trick mirror that multiplies the corners
of a room so that every spider hatches four,
I saw woodpeckers—a row of flames faltering
like candelabra. I'm brightened by intrusions,
pleased when I recall a hard name, when I find
a lost guest in the hallways of daydreams.
These brief visits seem honoring.
But when I turned to face him,
the branch sagged like a curtain wire
and my guest, that ruffled weight, was gone.
Later, while touching at chores
or sitting with my circle, those bored,
full-lipped duplicates,
the near, the far, the disappearing,
I heard his hammering, a battered alphabet
of one or two sharp consonants,
something prayerful and overworked
like chipping a long name upon a monument.
He tapped with tolerance, knocking
on the smoked glass of abandoned property.
I thought it was my door,
a door between two worlds.
Inspector of hollow hours, spy in a private ruin,
he reads lichens like small compasses,
the maps in wormwood where a few words
were chiseled. The bare trees left standing,
a spectacle, silvered,
more awakened than anything living.

The Pier

When I reached the harbor
the tour boats were sailing
out, others returning.
From a great distance,
people waved their arms
to whom, to what friends—
perhaps they saw the shore;
the shore is dear to all.
I like the way a pier ends
abruptly, madly, in the deep.
But here, useful ropes
are wasted as decorations,
the colored nets and floats
like discarded party favors.
I turn my back and rest
my full weight against the flat top
of the blackest piling.
The water's broken surface,
a looking glass that parts
the face from the body.
Strangers see I'm unhappy
and edge away, nearer
the concessions' bright awnings.
Is the sea jealous of the sky
or does the sky seek pleasure
in these twisting sheets?
White birds are mirrored,
or do gulls mimic
the rough wings of the surf?
I fell for it all,
two deceptions, the tides—
one that pressed close
its soapy veils, washing my name
from hers, and one that pulled back
leaving all creatures fluttering,
the squid's black word exposed.

The Continental Divide

I couldn't explain it to my husband,
who was squaring his papers as we drove
through the Carolina orchards.
So many ladders, left out in the rain
long after the picking season,
caught his attention, but the other
was a task to imagine. I pointed to the sign
that read Eastern Continental Divide
and lifted my foot off the accelerator
as we crossed over. The fields stretched easily
in both directions and there was no difference,
no natural landmark. He looked at the road ahead
as if he expected its surface to alter.
I told him we were talking about water—
this is where rivers change course,
where one source can divide, become two
and move off following opposite routes.
His eyes narrowed as he twisted an apple stem
until it broke away cleanly from the fruit.
It must be like the moon and tides, he said.
But I told him even the trickle from the tap
made its decision here, left or right.
Where does the rain turn as it falls
in half, parting like hair, and what happens
to someone who weeps in this zone?
We passed fields of winter cabbages,
a thousand rows twirling out in straight
lines no matter how you eyed them.
And how would these cabbages roll,
he smiled. Uneasy with new facts of science,
he feigned abrupt fatigue and laziness
when it was a matter of sadness.
His eyes no longer followed the zinc edge
of the horizon against that early winter sky.
In a far pasture, I saw two buzzards

circling a darkness on the turf.
A dead calf, I thought.
Whatever it was,
it rose and shook itself.
I watched until the heavy birds
unwound from their spiral
and flew apart.

Against Spring

Daffodils try sarcasm now,
along rivers, carelessly slouched
above dirty collars of snow.
One hidden, purplish bulb
regenerates more impudence.
All winter I was nourished by laughters
and sickened by names.
I loved my avenues deformed by ice.
Visitors, who came at risk,
found no one in, but I was there.
If cold memory walked a long way
and waited through night
upon the landing, I heard its tuneless
whistling from my chair
beside the arid reading lamp.
Outside a modesty heaped up
the way a virgin pulls her sheet
to hide her own repugnance. Even so,
the sun intensified, and hovered
in a dizzy ring. Its tepid glare
awakened even the minuscule;
the spiders unraveled their hammocks
and all resumed one lazy appetite.
I resisted spring,
its noxious little rains,
the reactivated worms and roots
which probe immovable things.
I praise the dullest sentiments
of stone, the pure indifferent matters
unblemished by this green.
A bird sings one rare note
out of boredom, an awful chirp
which fanatics like to think depicts
a certain loyalty or love's alarm.
And look, a girl pulls off the head

of her own daisy so foolishly.
Jealous December, buried beneath
exuberant mosses, I can't forget you.
Now ivy crawls over institutions
for the incurable, and gardens fatten
with wax. Let numerous societies
hold hands, the lilacs and bees perform.
I preferred the blank shoots of frost,
imperishable blossoms on my glass.
Not for love, its irritating greens and golds,
the Aprils, the Mays, will I change
my disposition—
when desires grow back and thicken
like grasses, and the little ants gather
beneath the stone.

Child Burial

I was ashamed to think of anything
while the others remained blank with formality
and sorrow, but the casket looked small
as a lunch pail left behind at a picnic ground.
A breeze lifted my hair, a swirling
I enjoyed when riding carousel horses.
Our circle was immovable and closed,
a severe crescent stiff as snow fence.
To show respect, I chose the frozen posture
I learned at school, when lining up
for vaccinations. I shivered as the family
stared, measuring my size and seeking features,
for somehow I resembled what was lost
and my presence suggested a queer rivalry.
It was difficult to keep still
as the day walked on, the shellacked box mirrored
swooping birds, the whole world spinning on it.
It must have been the hour when I daydreamed
in class because I could not follow
the relentless algebra of stones, dull rows
like chalkboards repeating a hard lesson.
I preferred the hothouse lilies
which smelled like Karo and candle drippings.
Then I tracked a distant cloud, a grey funnel
of rain that dangled like a stocking miles away,
but I did not look again at death or see
what it saw about me.
The priest closed his book upon a snowy tassel,
white as the glare of that moody winter, white
as silk bunting I'd seen at the mortuary.
It was not the same color as those ponies,
polished for summer and tethered
nose to tail like all the days ahead.

The Beautiful Illness

"Illness is a long lane. . . ."
— *John Keats*

I can't forgive an old theme
in spring. Powdered aspirin
on the lips of white lilies,
the antiseptic color
injected in these lawns
reminds me of a beautiful illness
but I can't imagine coming down with it.
I'm out walking in a mood; it shames me
that six or seven gloomy moths,
my pet irrationalities,
and all my nervous thoughts are after me.
The evenings are warm and busy,
an atmosphere of crowded sewing rooms
where they make the lace attachments
for homely wedding gowns.
I think of love, how it should be drowned
like a spider in a drop of water.
A dull, reluctant drizzle would suffice.
Something falls in other lives
like footsteps coming
or someone kicks a tin can
tenderly all night.
A careful loitering might attune me
to my needs when the cheapest expectation
seems too dear. With this in mind,
I paid for the last newspaper
with its torn headline
and read of a place where business
was booming, but the faces
on money looked so dejected
I flattered a cashier
who was going off duty.
Of course I was joking, I left
in a flurry. A circle of insects
laughed along with me, convulsed

in precise, lonesome amusement.
I give up telling the truth to any stranger
and I can't worry about women who knew me
when I was used as an example.
Last winter, pneumonia sent out love notes
to many. Now tulips ascend like fevers,
the dogwood solicits my sickest responses.
It's useless to blame this season
or the next, and I don't excuse my part in it—
those desires left stupefied in public hospitals.
Why does it matter, for love evoked so easily
was lost, thank goodness, beyond memory.

The Wilmington Courthouse

From the basement windows, I saw the statue
of Caesar Rodney, Freedom Fighter,
as I toiled with my probation officer.
A little snow was falling on the marble steps,
eye level, on the horse's sculpted mane,
and on the hero's bronze collar, much higher.
I could hear the chairs grinding above me
in family court where a mother wept,
a familiar, low whirring
like a sewing machine treadle.
I'd been arrested, locked in the weekend jail
after visiting a condemned building
on Ninth Street, an ignorable event
except for the snitchy flames of a minuscule fire—
a windowsill ignited beneath a homemade candle.
Some officers came by with a pot-sniffing dog,
its muzzle black and velvety
not unlike the stuffed pets left at home
upon the chenille bedspread. The one
or two real junkies, recently injected,
flopped down like rag dolls before the dog's
bright growl, its studious nuzzling.

Tuesdays and Fridays I left the high school,
took the bus down Market Street to Rodney Square.
A radio in my coat pocket, blunt, waxy
like a bar of soap, tuned to one singer,
a grainy voice that rushed and halted
as if running down the landings of a long stairwell.
From the bus I looked past the lines of traffic,
a touch of breath on the grimy window placed me
but I was invisible in that world, that day,
as it pitched in orbit; just the other evening
I circled my own street to all hours of the night

because I couldn't read the house number.
Inside, my room was curtained, swept,
with all its small possessions disappearing,
and every shade drawn down against
childhood's bright, flashpowder moon.

I sat face to face with my dressy social worker
but the blackboards overhead, those night skies
I was living by, revealed nothing to her.
It was easy to tell the truth of lies,
and refreshed, I lied in new directions.
I had a suspect home life for which I was never
blamed or pardoned—I just wanted to leave
that final winter when the neighborhood sidewalks
froze over so you could not read the awkward cursive,
the signatures, the tiny handprints of the children.

Outside, snow caught in the Greek lettering,
slants of ice fenced the busy filigree
until I saw the snow stop
and the sun returning at its downward edge,
red in the west where the day was not over,
where the trolleys strained upwards
and braked on the crests of hills.

The Sapling

Crickets slowed or increased
in warmth and plainness,
a pure seeking.
Milkweed, puffball, the king
dandelion and its slave, the sun.
All that fluff until evening
when silence ascended
like stinging, wings whirring
two high notes against the screen.
The house was new, its bricks
laid even like sensible words
spoken before children.
Letters arrived for my sisters —
praise from schoolteachers
and news of the boy
on tour in Korea.
My father returned late
to work in the garden
when the sun swelled
and lowered itself gently
as if in injury.
I stood by his basket; the grass
steamed, the weeds stirred
as if still searching.
A hole was made
for the leafless sapling
that, nursed along, recovered
and grew on carelessly.
Its permanence assured, it opened out
obstructing window views.
For years it grew,
the parlor dimmed, and other rooms
were overtaken.
All youth was blurred

and left exposed in winter.
It was the coldest shade,
its cunning ways confused the summer
light that never caught up to us
as we are now.
In that house, a spider's egg exploded
with secret force,
its large family, so many,
wandered every way
but always into darkness.

July 9th, Lying-in

The room faced south,
faced the wind from Narragansett Bay
and from farther—it was the arid,
chalk-clean air of ancient worlds,
of ruins kept in order by quiet laws,
the protected acropolis, that early doorway.
All that went before arrived in me
that evening, each true art
and every practicality—
tools that still work as when first made
out of stone, out of bronze,
then you, your rainy flesh,
like a fossil first rinsed in a bucket
and rinsed again by the light of day.

It might be coincidence,
something explained by science,
a biological oddity or red letter
in numerology, that power similar
to the suck of drains, the swirling
of cyclones which twist left or right
depending in which hemisphere
the soul turns up.
Whatever made your birth fall upon mine
that same hot day and the decades between us
has its meaning. I keep my eyes opened
to that time, the same moment when daisies,
fish, ice sculptures began to decline,
stink, dissolve away.
Not this, our name,
a red blur writing
of its own importance—
a warm scrolling
upon the index of each cell.

The Lake

There's something false to this—
it's all surface, a shard of sky,
and below that, one imagines
a wild unconscious slime.
Lovers come at twilight, in neutrality,
couples who hang their heads
as if forced into arrangements
with their own reflections.
Birds shift down, dipping,
but only their shadows are cleansed.
They are hunting bluebottles
and other transparencies;
love could not inspire
such endless activity.
I stand on the bank, its ragged
moss like a velveteen collar
torn away at the shoulder.
Looking across, I see the other half,
the other so much like this place
and my place in it.
The scalloped algae parts
and there we are, mirrored
like James' witches
standing shameless and possessed
at either end, the moonlight's
slack bed sheet beneath us.

Signature Music

He stood at the steel sink
scraping off flaky burls
and rusty filigree from oysters,
a grainy clatter against the hushing
vowel sound of the tap left open.
From the radio, the melody was sadder
for its tendency to sound scratchy and unlevel,
slow, then hurried as if a girl too weak
to turn the lever was cranking a Victrola.
Always, it was the sea behind the thin curtain,
the steady respirations of someone confined
to bed because of chronic malady
or some seasonal despair.
We heard the bay's warped surface whining
nearer; all its schools of fish, its sifting gels
and microscopic swellings added resonance.
I tried the bowl of my glass, wetting my finger
and in fast circles reached a warm, flat tone
which answered the foghorn at Long Point.
The calm between us was so great,
all external noise seemed wry and beautiful.
Linens snapped on the clotheswire,
a terse refrain in the dark.
Then, the speechless call from the lighthouse,
one metronomic measure of white light
repeated for the lost,
the same deaf swirl for those at shore.

Two

A Seaside Moon

When I last saw her, the air turned cold and ferrous,
a great hull shouldered the pier where we stood.
Its departure pitched the skiffs and dinghies
until the surface smoothed, finding its level.

I fell into the black creases of those docks,
and sank to the center of town
where I searched in every tavern,
and the sight of her white neck half-hidden
in my scarves, as I described it,
was known by so many.
Then I walked the beach parking lots,
where I wrote a grainy note in lipstick
across a car windshield.
A beseeching smear, written backwards,
legible to one whose key fit the starter.
Yes, I leaned so far into that cleft of reason—
but in the harbor, a boat cut the water;
its wake a beveled mirror
which lifted, flattened all reflection.

I watched the heavy wingbeats of oars
seeking the inlets, then the ferry
in its careful sea room
gained the channel, but it's simple
just to drift from a place
where we once firmly stood.
I saw numerals and names
stroked across the flinty waves,
a queer tremor
on the surface where a ship was lost.
I waited for the earth to turn,
to navigate the black surf overhead;
then, the grey bloom at morning
as I studied the shore

swept clean, the home we made,
where a row of weeds edged
the snarling hybrids,
where one moon increases each night
its single dose of narcotic.

The Improper Persons

I know there is fact without meaning,
details passed over and no regret
for them. Days seem to go sadly,
a windmill in the plain wind,
then a sudden gloom appears
like decayed wallpaper of inner rooms
when buildings are demolished.

A falling apart attracts sympathetic
crowds, a curious praise, as people
look up to lost souls wavering on ledges.
I only called attention to myself.
A small unhappiness enlarged, a tear
struck a word and the print swelled.

In the two homely pages left open
after a book is read, a story goes on.
I retired with a fascinating blame
underlined in green pencil,
the love scenes were unmarked
and lacked interpretation.

Perhaps I have loved the improper persons,
the strangers whose speech I have stolen,
whose words are embedded in the powders
and medicine capsules of love's doom.
It's hard to tell of it
without dreadful music and petnames
said in suffering.

I might go too far back to a room's
indirect memory, where we once met
formally. And at nervous crosswalks,
in the parallel urges of these streets

I feel it. Even now, when our story
is old, a word rewords itself
or a love invents more.

Each night is long,
longer than the shadow of its day.
The moon lost all authority
but for a minor glistening
from no official place.
Let dead worlds die out,
and a world gone mad, like this,
live up to its name.

On Massachusetts Avenue

Does it matter if a little drop of water panics,
if a drop of water shivers over a wide street?
I have felt such a thing on Massachusetts Avenue
just as the crowd from the Orson Welles Theatre
scattered across an intersection at disagreeable angles.
I heard a woman rehearsing for an examination;
her teacher held a clipboard like a tombstone
to his chest. Their words were numb and stylish
as they recited verse or mathematics in the twilight,
something monotonous requiring a few odd pauses.
I can no longer think in swerves or stillness
beneath this heavy day, this blankness like a marquee
for the disgraceful arts of living.
Tonight the sky is an unshareable philosophy
and nobody looks up after the movie,
after having seen some lovers break apart;
the screen, which afterwards went dark,
intensified the feeling.
Now the buildings lean too near, so near I might
invent desires going on inside the open windows
and all my unhappy souls reach out with their
    thimbles.
I dislike these streets filled with young optimists,
the amateur instructors in raincoats the texture
of dollar bills. One must remember the suicides
that fail like umbrellas that won't open,
the autumn leaves, those too glum to fall.
It's just a thought that floats up now and then
like a cloud above a manhole.
It's a relief the Samaritans are answering
their telephones on a jingle, and other alert citizens
are lifting the shutters of this city.
Even the rejected, the missing, those with no
    connections,
look up from the hard work of staying lost.
It begins to rain: lice falling off the angels of God,
stars infested with seed and kisses, the filthy

refreshment of dreams which calms all memory,
a good rain in which to soak a small infected spot.
It makes me think of our most wicked intentions,
wine spilled down the collar of a loved one,
life's cold origin in the sea,
of anything grim in the context of romance.

Arcata

No one was swimming, we walked the beach
wading through small spasms
where the tide circled like an old pet
deranged by infection. Waves choked
upon their tethers, halted far out,
too entangled to resume.
We pitied the deep, its unattended places
where life was willing but unlighted.

There was a restaurant built against
a rocky shelf, where the sea teased
the diners with an edgy monologue
of someone accused, confessing.
The tables teetered, the floor sagged
slightly, enough to please us.
As the day sank, night ascended
as if walking a steep ruin.
Nothing was level—a rough thought
pitched me further from the steady truth.

In the glass, I noted her likeness
superimposed upon the water
but the background shifted, convulsed.
We only mirrored love's conditions,
its rise and fall, its homeless kelp
towing stones through the sea.
A waiter brought us plates
and afterwards removed the shells;
I watched him toss all twelve
ironic smiles into the surf
from a small balcony.
We stayed long after dark had smoothed
a final ulcer from the surface.
I could no longer turn to it,

direct my gestures there, or tell
which half was lost and what part crashed
and crashed again, for God's sake, even now.

Memory

We are not mentioned by others,
never greeted by friends,
old lovers deny that it was ever serious.
We return to a place and follow
a mystery to its little hole.
The sky had no imprint, it rained
the way ink drips from newsprint
and we hid behind that year
as if behind a blank billboard.
Perhaps a cold observer
could have written an ending
to this, as seasoned journalists
identify faces at the windows
of a burning building
and only the names are saved.
It was long ago, and never recorded
on forms, an elegant suspicion
with no official blame.
A youth waves a gasoline rag
in our old neighborhood
where some workers played a radio
so they would not hear
our lovetalk, our relief
like the squeak of a pulley.
Now fire begins intense explanations,
and its tall alibi, the smoke,
as anything left too alone
becomes wrongdoing.

Useless Days

These are the useless days,
and in the calendar of heaven
there's nothing planned.
Deaths occur, somewhere, everywhere,
and who knows who belongs to whom?
In this city, marbles roll into open drains,
into the loveliness of lost things.
Such and such adds up,
so if I once burst into tears
in the reception area of a physician's office
it had nothing to do with my treatment.
The white light of medical places
keeps me alone; my name written on a form
seems plain but nurses stumble over it.
I forget the business going on,
the others whose lives have failed early,
whose hearts have given out.
I shouldn't complain, but I just can't check
my pulse enough. It's an informal question
and the question assures me.
It might have no meaning beyond its one meaning.
Let therapists build their homes upon me!
Today as I walked to work, I noticed a cement mixer
churning the ore for a municipal project.
They were widening a street
that seemed wide enough to me,
as if many things at once could possibly smash.
I wondered what happens to memos
written just before companies collapse,
who gathers up apologies sent to improper addresses?
As the sun lifted like a heavy glue
over the cold offices, I saw two women crossing
the street, holding the same handbag.
They appeared to be two great needs
sharing one desire.
Each form was familiar, each flesh,

and the little purse in between was glossy
as a mirror. I turned to my question;
I took my question by its little wrist, I said,
"Did you see that?"
The day, all days and recollections
replied, "Yes, we see." For a while, at my desk,
I was filled with gladness in the form of sickness.

Malady

1

I thought I loved but it was malady,
a fainting spell
in an overheated library.
I tried to examine the way
it happened: the text opened.
It's so complicated, even memory
reels from its intricacies
and cannot explain the past.
Neither nostalgia,
with its feathery touch, nor a dream's
severe logic is enough.

These shelves are high—
was it indecent to climb the ladder
with just these skirts on—
there, I found a small volume
with rococo endpapers
that became our undoing.
They say the soul has no gender
but I don't believe them,
these archives are scented with syrups
and aspirin bottles left open.

2

Day again, the sun rises:
an orange mood-elevating pill,
a pathetic window shopper
with only a penny to spend!
Today, pink light crawled like a rash
over me and I lay in bed, feverish.
The proper name might chill me
like a wet cloth for the forehead.
I'm too weak to accept visitors,
but beneath the vaulted ceiling,
the arcing structure of my delirium,

I seat her near the bed
beside my green water glass.

A thermometer's red bead traveled far,
but not far enough to free me.
Life went on: a pet's whiskers twitched
easily, involuntarily.
A bee circled a tombstone, a wreath of duty
around the granite lilies: "What I loved,
I loved for good reason."

Current Diaries

I had not dressed well, nothing covered me.
Nothing worn outside the body could refresh
the dark feeling or conceal its gesturings.
It was cocktail hour, that time of evening
when bottles are arranged on white tables
at the book-signing party,
when the sky too is white
except for a few streaks unwinding,
the time of night when new dressings
are applied at the hospitals.
I walked alone down Mount Auburn Avenue,
half a block behind the partygoers.
I was keeping apart from the forwardness
of the past, its piercing chitchat
and grief-struck monotones.
But one sad thought, in lime-green acetate,
caught up, twirled her evening bag
and tried to link her arm in mine.
These dead girls have shamefully cheap taste—
glossy sandals that tippy-tap
like a jealous chorus line thundering.
Then she opened her purse to show me
an old promise I had made, wrinkled like a hankie
around a snubby pistol. She demanded we go
someplace for champagne cocktails to celebrate
and I almost went along with it,
I was taken by the mincing toe-striker,
the delicate gait of such a whore.
Then I saw the bookstore window,
its stenciled glass, and there was my trouble
passing out autographs to the overly cologned,
linen-jacket crowd. Standing there,
beneath musky rows of shames and loves,
a mistake made years ago, wearing her rings
and showing off her curves.
The error with an hourglass figure

writing her signature.
I wanted that name for proof
like the first dollar that's made
still tacked on the wall after a bankruptcy.
I waited outside, fascinated by the lipstick
shade of such a lie.
But my brassy debutante tried to distract me,
circling like a tatter in the dizzy wind,
and like a love discarded kept near,
fluffing her hair in the absence of a mirror.
Then we heard someone saying,
"What an attractive dust jacket,
glazed to prevent fingerprints!" This lifted me
through five notches of laughter, my little imprint
laughed also, shivered in her dress the color
of crushed fireflies. Let the party go on,
let the wheels of cheese flatten.
We slipped away, paraded through old times,
unaffected by current diaries that list one name
so chronically. We got drunk, we sat together
on one barstool as if it were nothing.
An imperceptible feat of balance,
not a matter of clinging, or of love,
never a matter of leaving.

Violence

I put my hands on love's back
and shoved love far.
She was already going
but paused on the stoop, scolding.
She took back the gloves
she had wrapped as a gift
and left the bottle of wine
shattered on the grass
where we once let our little pets run.
The sun shed its platinum hair,
and the wind yapped.

That winter there was no trial,
only the snow settling on the benches
by the sea, and the sea so impartial
it made me feel guilty.
All the shrieking seasons followed—
spring, summer, fall calling out,
"There's the accused, still walking around!"
I tried to think of that year
as plowed earth, later the green swell,
finally the mowing away—
yet, our violent parting resumes
each daybreak, and at night
continues its ascension
up the grainy stairwell into dreams.
It is the clothing I remove,
my nakedness, my daily tasks,
the blank sun rising
level with these streets.

Three

The Stone

I drive peculiar routes to come this way.
Just yesterday, I coasted near
to see the house accented by candlelight
at dusk, the hour when family dinners
have begun. I didn't care.
Behind an unfamiliar fence, the grave
was there with all its morbid qualities
unchanged. Add to this an element of rain,
a perverse gloss
against the bare marble of one name.

Pumpkins rotted on those shoulders
every fall. A sullen stone,
in winter it was marker for the snow.
Children played near as if under
the strict guidance of a nun who taught
monotonous ciphers, the inventory *one*.
It cast a narrow shade across the lawn,
like an isolated bed inside a sickroom.

How immaculate it seems, and wastefully
quiet as night falls like a dollar
no one reaches for. From the window
of a room, someone disapproving pulls
a curtain. But memory insinuates so much
it leaves an impure touch upon the clearest thought.
Let each day sink here.

Whoever rests beneath that brutal word
was first to organize our punishments and rules.
I'm still scolded by unhappy laughters
from that house, even now,
in the small committee rooms, in the city
that grows upwards to escape.

With My First Husband

The heavy plates never cracked,
our coffee had the same black sheen,
the salt poured a fine, moderate amount
those days we ate together at a diner
by the Providence river
where a drawbridge was locked in one final
half-arc over the green water.
The chowder was thin, grainy,
but the crackers in glazed paper
snapped perfectly in half.
We did not yet know our universe
of wrongdoings, they were simple enough—
the breath we took, the days lost,
a few stars tacked to the black window,
those bright early thoughts of leaving.
Well meaning, uplifted and dazed
by the sixties, our childhood ended
in a hushed ceremony beneath an archway
of gladiola. But as I walked to the altar
I thought of a black horse without its rider,
boots fastened backwards to the saddle.
He still wore the prep-school ring
and toted binders from the university,
I openly displayed the thin bracelets
of girls who slit their wrists
in fancy asylum parlors.
Twenty years have passed
since we shared that bland fare
meant for the feeble.
The diner was razed one morning;
a backhoe scattered paper scraps,
ten thousand tiny pleated cups,
and all my empty thoughts for him.
The drawbridge hangs at the same
uncorrected angle; rusted, monolithic

in its awkward stillness.
On both sides, the road crumbles
towards the boarded toll booths.
As a ruin it is young,
it lacks the dust of bones;
but here and there our weathered petnames
and first pledges score the metal.
Now our daughter crosses
the divided days, the nights
pulled taut like a circus wire.

The Past

They were laying tar on the streets today
and tar on the roofs. Then the night,
the unsightly stars like a pocked face
and the face must be forgiven.
I sat down on the stones that are finished
and looked at the clouds
which are never complete
and which never rest easily with the moon.
I acted so lovesick.
I did not think about the past,
it thought of me.
Recollections infested the halls.
A spider planned an hour
around my dull activities.
Solitudes so slight walk diagonally
across the wall and strike the day,
even the corner of my room
leaned far as if to find another house.
It's easier to forget the dead
than to forget the living,
who might pass us in the street
and shudder with recognition.
Both groups ignored my inquiries.
My intention was to start immediately
at something's end, a disappearance
so lovely, I believed it was flirtation.

The Riders

One girl was thrown, her horse gone.
They watched it gallop a half mile
in one gracious sweep up the hill
where it grazed, shaking its head
as its bit grew wadded with grass.
She'd lost her retainer in the fall,
and searched the corn stubble
for the small pink scallop.
The other girl invited her
to ride double, and together
they approached the loose mare.
But it used its freedom to dizzy them,
bolting at angles and trotting
in ragged spirals behind them.

The mounted horse disliked their paired
illogical balance, and pulled his head
down to his breast to arch and buck.
It was nothing much, the girls laughed.
They touched their heels back
to its flanks and leaned hard,
increasing their pressure on its spine
and it went off at a smooth, contrite stride.
The thrown one was forced to hold on
to the other's small waist
and she kept her face down, close
to her rider's collar;
the blond hair smelled burned and sweet
from inexpensive bleach.

All afternoon they hurried the horse
over the dry fields, jumping low walls
where pheasants erupted from winter nests.
Resting once near a stream, neither dismounted.
They leaned forward and back

together, as one figure, one shiver,
letting the horse drink and drink,
and the reins fall until the leather
was soaking.

Each felt the weight of her own hips
increased by the other's.
One held the reins of the beast,
the other took the small wings
of her rider's rib cage.
The winter fields were acrid, yellow as sulphur,
but new grass was starting at the fenceposts
and along the brown river.
At dark, they watched the flaring highway
for the headlights of their fathers' cars
until the yellow beams swelled, churned
with the rich dust of the paddocks.

Drugstore with Black Dolls

At my father's warehouse, I fell
as I climbed a pegboard
to lift the pages of a men's calendar.
My scrapes were raw, unsightly,
and the bookkeeper,
pleased to leave her chair,
took her cigarettes and Zippo
for the walk to the pharmacy.
The store was narrow, deep,
a fan with two long streamers
whipping at the entrance.
The dolls were tall as true children,
boxed, tied with pink cellophane sashes
and arranged in gradation like a choir
above rows of gauze and iodine.
I couldn't move closer,
there was something about the lamps
that flickered when the fan
rotated left, then jolted right.
I was alarmed to see the world
had needs beyond my own, beyond my first
longings for a flaking china doll
my mother's mother owned and handed down.
Whoever made these dolls never
thought of me! And I couldn't think
of owning one or kissing her
at twilight riding the glider
as my brothers watched.
Yet, jealousy has an irritating touch
like the ribbon on the fan,
and it caused me to take an inventory
of my collection left at home:
a doll that cried salt water
if I filled her with an eyedropper;
a lead soldier, a red crosshatch

on his breast pocket; an Arabian horse
its mane torn in velvet lines —
these didn't please me
once I had seen black dolls.
They were not beautiful, their clothes
probably flammable, and tight red lips
chipped easily at my touch. I was disturbed
by pleasure, same as dropping paper
on the surface of a fast river.
I knew as the earth turned
half of it was dark
and half was light.
The dark assumed the anonymity
of something misplaced
without an owner's search for it.
I thought of those dolls at night,
beneath the heavy linen of dream;
a world turned evenly, increased,
and the deep I wished to learn
washed over me.

Church Work

The church was clean with the purity
of places never slept in, never left open
to nights, or to those out walking.
In spring it smelled of starch
when women wore linen.
Tombstones in the tiny historic plot
leaned different ways like ironing boards
askew. The Sunday light clothed everything,
streets and sidewalks in bleached muslin.
At twelve, she was too sullen to sing
and refused to rise from her place,
a walnut bench difficult to scar
without a knife or bottle cap.
The choir performed out of sight,
almost out of hearing as she stared
at the high window at the end,
the small lesions of glass
in which the light was marred and frozen.
Her father watched ahead, listening,
ready to follow the broader guidelines,
but she focused on tree houses, rope ladders,
water towers, whatever climbed higher
than that steeple.
She thought of wide fields, electric fences,
places where she could tear her clothing,
the Delaware with its poisoned edge,
a spill of mercury through the cattails,
any clear route the soul takes to escape.
She was nourished by daydream, commanded
to evade her lessons. To think of God,
she imagined closing a seam,
bringing in others' ruined mending.
It was better to cross the slags,
to trail the city's changing outskirts
where life was steady exploration,
a sane, methodical freedom.

In Back

Trampled chive, dandelion
sharpen the breeze at twilight
as I watch two youths
at dark, near summer's end
when the inseparable uncouple
and begin to ward off one another.
Like oysters, mussels, a sea life
that grips and pulses through
the short grass, they halt
as one-closed flesh.
The fight is even, neither gains
and it turns awkward when one
upon the other grinds his hips
and face to face exchanges breath,
his oaths slurred, strained,
faltering like vows.
A moment, at first so effortless,
grows forced, bewildering,
until their color changes tone,
shifts and deepens
as when debts are told or a dream
is confessed in broad daylight.
The sun twirling down behind
the westside roofs, like a foil balloon
in a dance-lesson studio,
exaggerates the red in everything.
Soon the circle of sisters, the fathers
still dressed in wingtips, white-shirted,
are stirring. Seeing no blood,
the group breaks apart as if leaving
until someone says "Kiss him!"
In the nearest kitchen, plates click
against the bare Formica.
We wait for one error, that swooning
at night's abrupt ledge

from which the day falls.
Then I saw it, a bright spill
as the two rocked forward,
rolled apart, bruising
the onion grass
until the air burned.

1917

She took the short route to her place of work
past the children's home, where she'd left him
for good, as one might turn a pocket inside out
to remove a paper wrapper or a seed.
She showed a new severity of dress,
wearing new business clothes
without the scalloped apron he remembered.
She could not walk far enough
to disappear completely, and in a small mirror
of polished slate, he chalked her picture.

His father dead, she searched
mattresses and underneath the floorboards
but nothing was saved, only nests
of blistered foil and cellophane.
At the office, men admired her hands,
unblemished by her brief chores at mothering,
and by her husband's illness
which ended quickly beyond her touch.
She never advanced in her work;
the ledgers were awkward, unruly in her arms.

His father might have held him; his coat
was fireproof, large enough to hide them both.
He dreamed of it: an orphan riding the hook and
    ladder
in the blood-poisoned arms of a ghost.
But it was she who approached, parading
along the high fence of his youth.
No charity, no trade learned in the state system
gave him skills to smooth the raised grain
of a father's coffin.

His finger traced a worn and beautiful psalm
until the print lifted off, into him.
All days started with her receding figure;
as she walked away her attire grew darker.
Years passed, each with its back to him.
At last, he saw her silhouette
against the kitchen wall in childhood,
its ragged features of scrap paper,
the warmth from the grate increasing.

The Voice Lesson

Walking down that street, she felt like a pea
teased forward on the blade of a knife.
The sidewalk was steep or it was the angle
of some mood that threatened her.

Ah, happiness, your ankle is broken!

High up, a window washer waved a stinging rag
signaling some suicides perched at different levels.
No one followed through with it. So many glum
constructions, each with a bad purpose:
at noon, a big clock prayed on the church roof.
It must have been payday, the way people acted.
Men walked the way men walk with cash on them,
and girls circled the public fountain
watching the water churn their soiled wishes.

Nothing's worth a penny to me, she thought,
as she watched the locksmith duplicate keys
for some hospital workers, for the closet
with the morphine elixirs.
Next door, a clerk tore the dress from a mannequin.
One arm unscrewed, the dummy rocked on its
    pedestal,
its glossy waist was beautiful.
What scenes, what scenes from what memory?

Salesmen carried the white mice of their names
in shiny coat linings and whispered company slogans
which were slightly erotic.
I'm just taking a walk without any money, she said.
Then the mayor came out of city hall
toting a large scissors; a child shadowed him
with a spool of gold ribbon, a piece so wide

it might hold back the tangled hair of angels
and all those left unattended in heaven.
It must be a new business opening,
but when she followed them there
it was only a hole in the ground
and a crane with its neck hanging.

It's good commerce to own the sun
and owe to one moon.
Also, there's the cheap publicity of rain,
the several selling points of stars.
Even so, billboards are peeling, perhaps
the best use for time-lapse photography.
She reached a place where someone
took a voice lesson. The tune was odd,
a formless wavering, and like the day,
a note held much too long.

So she knew it was a drunk at practice
or someone too lonesome to keep quiet.
Thank God There Is No God, a stern vibrato
accompanied by a crescendo of sharp instruments.
It's just the barber with a customer.
But who is this coming?
The boy who sweeps the clippings off the stoop
as if it were everything, everybody's earnings,
a vile tangle, proof of God.

Discreet

Today I wrote the ending of all poems.
It came like a strict rain
in an impersonal tone, with the awkward marks
and small corrections of stars at night.
I unlinked the pendant from its chain
like an intimate word once fastened to a phrase.
There were inexcusable vowels,
a slurring beautiful lie.
Now rhymes fall to their knees
upon sharp glass, and a name rides bareback
out of sight.
I might tell a word too long to tell,
inform without information,
but I won't let a dream repeat itself
in a story.
I autographed my wish and gave it
to another, but it was whiter than paper.
I can no longer spell the truth,
its one pure syllable,
or read myself to sleep
beneath dim lamps.
All unfinished days,
the formless, incompleted loves
have fallen to one corner of a page,
a loveliness or error
where the ink has deepened.

Ball of String

Behind the lettered windows
where they work for death,
I made a will, a small one
with her name.
A concentrated ink dimmed
the swirling offices
until a notary exposed his wrist,
that glaring cuff link sent by God,
a sad, officious star.
It made me think I won't assign
my cluttered days,
I'd rather offer restlessness
or wit, a good riddle or a joke
that lives long after telling it.

Tonight the electricity went off;
the dark directed me through rooms.
Our house was disassembled, ruined
by shaky moonlight
as I numbered all the chairs.
Seated there, my heavy family,
my thoughts, stood up and left me.
A portrait of myself in a bad mood
can't be of use, and no sense naming
this and that for them!
I'm more inclined to list each little burn,
the highball circles on the wood,
all memory's bleached surfaces.

I had to face my daughter's face
and the tiny corners
of our photographs taped against
the sky's black paper.
Tell her life has no true order:
a ball of string. The grasses

and the rains weave temporary shapes
like souls untethering from the flesh.
Let collectors come, the humorless prowlers,
yard sale buyers, truth seekers!

I have too many papers.
Pierced upon the narrow spindle
of each day, the letterheads
and imprints of all the wrong people.
Even my notes returned unopened
as if I had sent them to accuse myself.
Yet, in a calendar marked by instructions,
in desires rationed out
with humanity's sameness,
a willingness, milky and phosphoric,
increases in its outlines.
Airy ghoul, well meaning —
the near-death of all loves —
come close, allow me this,
then fade like scent
as we walk these rooms.

About the Author

Maria Flook was born in Hamilton, Ontario. She has published two other books, *Reckless Wedding*, her first book of poems, for which she received a Great Lakes Colleges Association New Writers award, and *Dancing with My Sister Jane*, a book of short stories. She has been a writing fellow at the Fine Arts Work Center in Provincetown, and received an NEA fellowship in poetry writing in 1988. She has taught at Rhode Island College and Roger Williams College, and now teaches part-time at Warren Wilson College. She lives in Asheville, North Carolina.

About the Book

This book was composed on the Mergenthaler Linotron 202 in Garamond No. 3. Garamond was introduced in America by ATF in 1919, when their cutting, based on the *caractères de l'Université* of the Imprimerie Nationale, appeared. Many other versions were made by the English and American Linotype and Monotype, by Intertype, Ludlow, and the Stempel Foundry. It has been adapted for phototypesetting, CRT typesetting, and laser typesetting.

The book was composed by Marathon Typography Service, Inc., Research Triangle Park, North Carolina, and designed and produced by Kachergis Book Design, Pittsboro, North Carolina.

WESLEYAN POETRY, 1990